Sj Conerly

Sj Conerly

Scared of Butterflies

Sj Conerly

Copyright © 2019 Sonia Conerly

All rights reserved.

ISBN: 978-0-692-11022-5

Sj Conerly

DEDICATION

To my sweet, soft spoken beautiful big sister Shawne, thanks for believing in me and loving me unconditionally.

Sj Conerly

Stage One
An Egg

Chapter One
My Beginnings

Beginning, *the point in time or space at which something starts.........*

In the beginning, my process was easy because I was in my mother's womb. I had no difficulties but was now born into this world unprotected from life's lessons. My journey through my beginnings in life was as if I was drilling through the core of the Earth. I knew my mother wanted the best for her baby girl. I knew she prayed that I would have a good life, that God would bless me, and that I wouldn't have rough beginnings, but life does happen. We don't know the life that God wants us to journey through. The pathways won't always be straight. They could have lots of twist and turns as we journey through them. We sometimes repeat the same things in life, going in a circle until

Sj Conerly

we learn from those lessons.

    We never ask for who our parents are going to be. I believe God picks your parents, no matter their flaws, for your make-up. I was born to two people God wanted to create me. I was born to my beautiful mother and my father who was a pastor, and they made a beautiful, bouncing baby girl that my mother named Sonia McNeal. I was a baby that moved fast. I was told that I started crawling and walking early. I wasn't a talkative child, but I was an inquisitive one. I can remember getting fussed at by my mother for being in adult conversations. I did things that got me into trouble. One of my siblings would get into trouble for things that I did. I was a spoiled child and that's something that hadn't changed, not even now. I laugh when I think about it. I do like my way sometimes, but the part of me that can be mean, I didn't like. You never know the hand you're going to be dealt in life. I believe as children we all have big dreams that we just know we're going to achieve. Achieving my goals was something I always thought about. Something I'd always wanted, but my process as I was growing into this butterfly was difficult and challenging. A butterfly is beautiful, but it goes through an ugly process to get that beauty; my process was ugly. I was trying to get to that butterfly. I was trying to get to that beautiful stage. The ugliness hurt; it felt like a hundred bees stinging me at one time. My process in life had been rough, sad and lonely at times. As I got older, I thought the hurt, pain and ugly process would dwindle. I thought the pain would reduce, I thought things would get better in my life, but it got harder and more painful as I was trying to grow into a butterfly.

Growing up without my father in my life was a hard process for me to live with. Many times, I didn't know how to feel when it came to my father. My emotions would be all over the place, very unstable at times. I didn't know the extent of the relationship between my parents, only what I'd heard about the relationship and my father. I never was told much about him, only that he was a country bumpkin. I knew nothing to relate to him; I didn't even know if I looked like him. I can remember a lady that I used to go by to buy frozen cups from, told me out of the blue one day, "You sure have them McCann legs." I would just look because I didn't know who McCann was. What was a little girl supposed to say to she has legs like McCann? I thought about who McCann was when I left her house. Maybe it was somebody that was in my family on my mother's side, or maybe it was somebody that she knew that my legs reminded her of. I was the little girl with the McCann legs, the little girl that thought deep about my McCann legs as I walked up the street home. I told one of my siblings. I looked down at my legs and thought, whoever McCann is, their legs sure are pretty. The next time I went to her house to buy me a frozen cup I was running down the street fast as I could because it was hot and I was trying to keep up with my sister as she ran; she was so fast. We ran up all the stairs to the door. The old lady looked at me once I got to the door and told me to, "come in child." When I walked through her door she said, "you look just like your daddy and you know you have them big McCann legs." I smiled the biggest smile ever because I never met my father and she knew him. From then on, I would look at my legs and would say I have legs like my daddy. I was proud to have big legs like him; happy to know anything that I could relate to when it came to him. My mother never talked about him, never even told me his name, even though she said she did, but if she did, I didn't remember that. I was about six or seven at the time when the frozen cup lady told me this information that my mother hadn't. As a little girl, I wanted to know him and when she gave me that little bit of something that was so big to me and meant so much, I was ecstatic. I started going to her house just to hear her tell me that I had McCann legs; my daddy's legs.

****

Life started to change for me when I was about eight years old; I didn't understand why at the time. I just knew that it was changing and not in an effective way. By the time I turned nine years old, I was blossoming as a young girl. I was a tomboy, always playing with the boys, playing football better than them, running faster than them. I had big dreams; my light was shining as bright as the stars. I felt even though my mother was on drugs now and even though I had no lights, no water, no food to eat at times, I knew I was destined to do something great. I knew God had a greater plan for me just like I heard in church, but my process was really getting ugly.

One day waiting on my mother to come home, I guess she was going to get my little sister and I something to eat. My sister kept telling me she was hungry, so I brought her to the bathroom and told her to think about her favorite food and drink the water until her stomach felt full. We both drank water from the faucet until our stomachs felt full. After that, I took her back to our room laid her down and not long afterwards, she was asleep. I went and laid down too, waiting for my mother. My other siblings weren't home, and my mother never came back home. I got up and looked out the front door looking for my mother, but I didn't see her. I knew not to go outside at night because if my mother or one of my siblings caught me, I would be in trouble. So, I just closed the front door and locked it back. When I turned around to go back to the room, I saw a man seating on my mother's bed; it was her friend Stanley. He told me to come here and I walked over to him. When I got to him he told me to come closer, so I did. He picked the lotion up and told me to rub some on his stomach for him. I got scared because it didn't feel right for me to be doing that. He put some lotion into my small hand and I began to rub it on his stomach as I was told. Then I felt what I knew was his man parts on my arm; I was scared. At nine years of age, I knew that I wasn't supposed to be rubbing lotion on his stomach, but I was too scared. I wanted my mom, but she wasn't there, my siblings weren't there, my daddy wasn't there. At that moment, I wished I was with my dad, I wished someone was there to help me. He made me do things that I didn't need to be exposed to. I couldn't tell you how long I was in my mom's room with her friend, but it felt like a lifetime. After a while, I told him that I was tired, and he told me that I could stop. I went in my room and laid back down, wanting my mom to come home badly. I must have fallen asleep because I was awakened by him touching me between my legs. I jumped up and he said, you peed that bed. I guess me peeing in the bed saved me from whatever else he had planned for me. I was afraid. I can't remember if I cried. I looked over at my sister and went to lay down with her. I didn't change my nightgown because if he came back in the room, I'd still be pee-pee. When I laid next to my sibling, I thought, thank God it happened to me and not her. I felt I saved her from getting hurt, I saved my little sister from an emotional roller coaster. That day, I vowed to protect her from anyone that would try to hurt her. I would be there for her whenever she needed me.

Chapter Two
Trying to See the Stars

Trying, *difficult or annoying; hard to endure.........*
Star*, a fixed luminous point in the night sky which is a large, remote incandescent body like sun.........*

Telling this part of my life, I didn't mean to hurt anyone. I was hurt; it's my life, my truth. I know that some people can't handle the truth, my truth, that they were a part of. My life's little scars that were afflicted on me. Scars that made my process of becoming a butterfly harder. This was the effect of me trying to get through this process.

My changing period of my life was getting difficult. The process was getting scary. I noticed that we weren't eating like we should have been, and we started moving a lot more than normal.

Scared of Butterflies

My body started to change more and more, and people let me know it. My body wasn't something I was into. I was so young I didn't know what fine was. I always heard that I was fine, but I didn't understand what people meant by saying it. Until they would say something like, "you are fine with that big butt to be so young." So, I guessed me having a big butt equaled to fine. I would hear that so much from people that I didn't know, and people that I did know. People closer to me noticed my body changes and would tell me more often than I wanted to hear. Sometimes I wanted to scream out and say, it's more to me than my body. I'm a smart girl I can do all kinds of crazy tricks with my body like a gymnast. I wondered why those things weren't highlighted more than my butt.

    I just knew I was going to become a gymnast, but we couldn't afford the lessons. My sister Carmen introduced me to track and field and I was hooked instantly from the first practice. Running was like a drug; it numbed everything for me, it calmed me. I was happy that running and I found each other at a time that my life was changing. I didn't know why at the time, but I knew it was. Running became my best friend. I was so young that I didn't know why things were happening.

My innocence as a child was more likely the reason that it sheltered me, until nothing could protect me from what my eyes saw, and my ears heard. A child's innocence should be protected, and no one should have robbed me of it. My siblings and I moved with someone we knew. I can't say if he loved me, all I knew was that I didn't feel loved. My family had been torn apart and that's all I could see. I knew my mother was on drugs, and I noticed that people we knew treated us differently because of it. I saw the praising of my cousins and not me and my siblings, the negative talking about me acting as if I didn't have feelings.

Family members would call my sister Carmen

in the room and make fun of the way she talked; she had a soft, sweet voice to me. I had learned at a very young age to develop tough skin. I'd dust the words off my shoulders like it was nothing. I was hurting on the inside, but I wouldn't dare show it. I wouldn't allow anyone to have the pleasure of seeing me hurt. However, it wasn't helping me mentally. My home life was being affected by something debilitating; but I didn't know what it was.

I didn't know then why the decision was made for us to go live with this person, but I did know that I wished I could have just stayed with my mother or perhaps if she knew where my daddy was I could've lived with him, but most of all, I wanted my mother. I needed her; there was nothing like the love from your mother. It's warm and caring, it's something that you just want as a child. I longed for my dad and wanted his love, wanted him to show me that he loved me. I wished he had love for me; I hoped he loved me even though he didn't know me.

Maybe that was just wishful thinking as a child, not understanding why your father wasn't in your life, and on top of that, my life was crumbling right before my eyes.

After living there for a while, a big fight happened. I didn't know who made the call, but it was told that we weren't being taken care of. I knew things were different and to hear when someone got mad and told you to take off clothes that you had on, was humiliating. To know you had near to nothing had to be hard for my sibling. I was a little girl so maybe it was my little girl mind wondering? I'd heard someone say that person didn't get any money to take care of us, but whatever reason it was, we should have been taken care of. Not just with things. A child needed that financial stability, but they needed to be nurtured and showed that they were loved. I didn't get that. Maybe he didn't know that no love was being shown to me.

I can remember that we were taken from that family friend. Carmen and I went to live with someone else we'd known for a while. I liked it there. I remember before school we would have had to say our prayers and when it was time for bed. I was taught how to sit and eat correctly at the table. I was told that girls are sugar and spice and everything nice. I liked that, but I was a tomboy and I liked to play in the dirt and play with the boys. Most of all, I felt the love that came from him. Not long afterwards, Carmen left to go live with a friend. I can't remember when I left that home of love and ended up back with my mom, but not long after, I was back with the first person they had taken us from. I didn't like living there again and I wanted and needed my mother. No matter what, no one could replace your mother, and that's who I wanted to be with.

Sj Conerly

****

Living back in this home, I didn't know what to feel. I loved my mother, but she wasn't there to tell me she loved me back. I wanted that love, I needed that, because this house was the no love house. I was motherless, fatherless. I didn't know my father, so it wasn't the same as how much I missed my mom. I missed her touch. I missed her combing my hair, even though she didn't know how. I even missed her whipping me when I did wrong.

I needed my mom, especially went I started my menstrual. One night my stomach started hurting bad, so I went upstairs and went to bed. The next morning, I had blood in my little girl underwear. I went to tell the person I was living with that I got my period. She told me to go get a clean pair of underwear, then she rolled some tissue up and pinned the tissue in my little girl panties and told me to come to her job on my way home from school, so I could pick up the pads. Now at that age, I didn't know what to do or how to take care of myself with a period; the month before I'd just turned ten years old. Looking back on that, I wonder why I didn't get the talk about what to do and what it meant.

I remember when my daughter first got her period, I had a talk with her about it and before she got her period, I talked to her letting her know what it meant and that ever young girl got a period, why she needed it, and how to take care of herself with it. My niece that lived with me I had the same talk that I had with my daughter. I wondered then why me, why I didn't get that talk? My mom wasn't around. I thought then, was it because I'm not his wife's daughter? What was wrong with me? I had to learn on my own. I know that may seem small to you, but for a ten-year-old, that was a big milestone in my life that I had no one to talk to about, getting my period and becoming a young lady. I didn't know what to do. Maybe she was waiting for my mom to have that talk with me. I wished my mom was there. I knew it would have been different.

This time of my life, I didn't remember having many good memories. I remembered being sad and wanting my parents a lot. I wondered where my daddy was, and I couldn't remember the last time I had seen my mother. I was missing and needing my mom, wanting my dad. My very first time meeting him I was eight-years-old.

I hadn't seen my siblings; at that time in my life, I didn't know where my siblings were.

I wished we would see each other again soon.

I wanted my siblings around like we used to be. I knew three of my siblings were in New Orleans, I just didn't know where the other two were. I didn't know why we all weren't together anymore. It was only me that was there living with him now. I was this sad little girl with no one to lean on, no one to talk to anymore.

My older siblings were my best friends and

losing your first best friends isn't easy when they are your siblings. My mind would always wonder about different things, but mostly it would be about my life and how I could come up with a plan to get us back together. I came up with a plan to get one of my older siblings to come get me and then maybe we would all be reunited and living together again as a family. Maybe my mom would never leave us again if she saw all of us together, because I missed her so much.

    I stole something that was of value and hid it, but, then I thought someone would find where I put it and that would destroy my plan, so I hid it in my panties. When the friend of my family that I lived with asked me did I see what I knew I had stolen, but he didn't, that's when I put my plan into acting. I lied and told him that I saw my brother in his room messing around his dresser. It's not verbatim, but I know it was in that way. I wanted my brother to come get me. I just knew the plan I came up with would work. And I knew when my brother saw me that he would take me with him. I knew my brother had to miss me like I missed him. That's why I stole, not for myself, just to get my brother to come and take me with him. I think our family friend I was living with went looking for him, but he showed up at his house while he was gone. I was so happy; I just knew that I was leaving that day. My heart was beating with joy because I was finally leaving the house of no love. After all, how I was looking all nappy head and clothes looking a mess, that didn't compare to how my inside was feeling. I felt ugly, I felt useless, unwanted. My brother came and left; he didn't take me with him that day. I guess he didn't want me, just like my parents. My little girl mind was everywhere. Feeling unwanted was an emotion that at such a young age, I shouldn't have been feeling.

    Now, I'm not saying that family friend didn't do his best with me, but as a child, I felt alone and unloved. Sometimes I felt that I should have been in foster care if I wasn't getting shown any love. At least in there, there would be no pretend. I'm not saying that, that family friend didn't love me, he just didn't show it. After a while, I was used to the no love being shown. I was so angry I can remember fighting one of my aunties. I don't know why I wanted to call her and ask her why we had a fight, so I could write how it made her feel that her little niece fought her, but I felt she might not remember or she would take it the wrong way so, I'm moving on.

I didn't want to put in this book like I was all good, because I wasn't. The bad side of me was silent at first; on the inside, the anger gradually grew. The little girl crying on the inside. No one to express the hurt I was feeling internally. I was an egg needing protection, but I was growing and developing into dark colors; the brightness was being shaded in colors that I didn't recognize. Things were happening on the inside mentally that I didn't understand as a child. I didn't have anyone that I could ask about how I felt and to explain the thoughts of confusion that were going on. My growth slowed down, and at a young age, I was an egg being attacked by every dangerous predator that was creeping and crawling.

Scared of Butterflies

Chapter Three
My heart Hurt

Hurt, *cause physical a pain or injury to*.........

I don't know when we went back and stayed with my mother. I do remember losing my paw-paw and then one of my brothers was shot in the head as my sister Carmen and I sat outside on the steps of my cousins' house. My brother and his friend were racing on the bikes and a close friend of the family told them to stop. I thought, he's older than you. How could you tell him to stop racing on the bikes? Now that I'm was older, maybe that friend felt something.

When the shots rang out, his friend racing on the bike with him ran, saying my brother's name and that he was shot. My mind went blank for a minute or so. I can remember seeing him trying to get up off the ground and screaming I can't see. Even though he survived that tragedy, that day my brother's life changed forever. It was a very sad time in my life, and I was hurting eternally for my brother. He was so young and now had to live with a disability which had to be hard. He never really lived to his fullest potential; a young man that never was able to grow his wings and become a butterfly.

Scared of Butterflies

Chapter Four
Incapable

Incapable, *Unable to do or achieve (something)..........*

This part of my process destroyed the little girl in me. This butterfly affect had altered my thinking, and my thoughts about men. My ability to grow was slowing down. It's hard for me to write about this part of my life. It brings up the ugliest part of it that damaged my ability to truly and fully love and know what real love felt like. All I could remember was hurt in my life and because of this, the good times I had slowly started to leave my memory. I was a ten-year-old girl the day I was raped. I couldn't understand why this sixteen-year-old boy did this to me. Maybe if I would have had the strength to say stop, he wouldn't have raped me, or if I would have had the courage to tell someone he would have gone to jail, but I was so scared. I didn't move, I just laid there. When he pushed his way inside of me, I saw a new world of something different; it felt strange. I can't really explain the feeling. All I wanted was for it to be over. I was a ten-year-old girl, but my body wasn't shaped as if I was a little girl. If you just looked at my body you would have thought I was way older at my age, so I guess I deserved what was happening to me or maybe I did something to bring this on myself, I thought. I didn't call out for help; I didn't ask God to help me. I was numb at what was happening but when it was over, I was in pain. I can remember my vagina hurting for days, a reminder of what happened to me, and that wasn't the only time he raped me. I was afraid of him at this point. He even told people he had sex with me. No one came to my defense and said you had sex with a ten-year-old girl. People in our neighborhood knew I was ten-years-old. The women talked about me and the young guys and men wanted to have sex with me even more. There was no more secretly trying to make sexually advances at me. I was so ashamed of what happened to me. Now once again, in my life a man was violating my body. I felt I was going crazy I wanted the act to be wiped out from my mind and out of my life as if it never happened. So, I allowed people to believe I had sex with him rather than any of them knowing he raped me. I know that doesn't sound right, but rape made me feel ugly, confused and alone. I felt as if I was closed in a tight space of darkest hugging on to me so tight that I couldn't move nor think straight. I don't know when and I don't know how I blocked it out but, I did. At first, I never told anyone about what happened to me. I let that part of me die deep into my memory, buried never to be dug up again. I thought no one would believe me anyway. I was being called hot and fast because I had a body like a woman and because of that I thought people would say I asked for it or just wouldn't believe me. So, I let it die along with my self-esteem, my self-confidence and my self-worth. I believe

I stop loving myself that day, it was a very familiar feeling that I knew all to well.

I felt ugly, I looked ugly, I would think to myself. Although at the time, I didn't understand how it would affect me. Sometimes I really didn't want to understand; I was very confused. I knew I wasn't a woman, but somehow my eyes were open in a way they shouldn't have been. I was sad, hurt and scared.

This process stagnated my life at the age of ten. I began to grow even more angry than before. Life wasn't dealing me a great hand at my youthful age. I was still an egg, still growing. I was not in my mother's womb being protected, not a baby, but a pre-teen that was still trying to understand a lot of things that were happening in my life. My beginnings; I wasn't even in act two when things started to divulge in a way they shouldn't have. I was a young girl, only on this earth for ten years, and look at the things that were happening in act one. When I should have been seeing things that little girls saw. I shouldn't have been going through these things. At a time like this, I needed my dad. I hadn't seen him in two years, even then that was my very first time meeting him, and I didn't know if I would see him again. Wherever my dad was, I needed him more than he knew. I needed to feel protected as if I was on the inside of my mother's womb. I did have an older brother who was like a father to me, but he never came around anymore. My second oldest brother was here but not like he used to be since he got shot. I thought, why God didn't save me from act two? I had a climax in my life already, and not in a good way. I knew my mother prayed that I would have a good life, that God would bless me and that I wouldn't have rough beginnings, but life happened. In my beginning, my process was easy because I was in my mother's womb. I had no difficulties, but now I was born into this world unprotected from the dangers that exist and life's lessons.

  We don't know the life that God wants us to

journey through. The pathways won't always be straight through this journey. There will be a lot of twists and turns and sometimes going in a circle, repeating the same things in life, until we learn from the lessons. I just didn't know how me being violated would teach me a lesson that would be fulfilling to my life. I was too young to truly understand the trials of life, and that God had a plan for me.

Chapter Five
Birthday

Birthday, the anniversary of the day on which a person typically treated as an occasion for celebration and the giving of gifts.

I was so happy the day once I turned thirteen. I don't know why I just was. On that day, my school had a half of day. When the bell rang I left class in a hurry and ran two blocks to the bus stop. I was so happy running to the bus stop, maybe because it was my birthday, but I felt something was going to be different that day; something in my life was going to happen in a good way. I very seldom felt positive feelings. My mind would always think of things that I wanted to happen because my life was so different, my process in my youthful years was so problematic. Once I made it home, there was no happy birthday, no cake, no balloons, just an apartment that was full of disappointments that was numbed by drugs and alcohol. A place that I wanted to escape.

Things in my life continue to go down a down wood spiral. I was taught by my mom to pray about everything, but in these times, I wasn't doing much praying.

Crack cocaine, is a form of drug that has been purified and made into crystals.

The crack epidemic.

This small piece of rock that gave a short intense high bulldozed my family structure. I saw the destruction of families, my neighborhood and I was right in the middle of the tsunami trying to swim and navigate my way through to survive it. I needed a way out, and I had it with my first love, track and field. I worked hard at it. Sometimes it was difficult to concentrate on running and school work when you were hungry. It was hard to deal with everyday life more often than it should have been. My thoughts were more all over the place, and I was slipping in and out of my pretend world more now than normally. I was trying to understand what was going on with me. I couldn't remember why I was hurting when I was in my pretend world until it manifested into my life. Most times I couldn't even remember the good times. I was losing memories that I should want to know. Even though I knew I wanted more than the environment I was in. My dreams of me being this big track star started to change. I stated to lose the good parts of me. I was doing things that could have landed me in jail or dead. I even tried to set a man on fire with a lighter and a can of hair sheen. Yes, he was being disrespectful to me in ways that I didn't deserve, but what if I would have succeeded and set him on fire? I'd probably be on death row right now or serving a life sentence. I would be remembered as this angry girl, who had a troubled childhood, that set a man on fire for disrespecting her, then I would have been forgotten about. No one would be speaking on the trauma that was done to me years before, or me having daddy and mommy issues.

    I didn't succeed in setting that man on fire. I was angry, and that anger could have gotten me killed. That same man came to my mother's house to kill me, but I wasn't there. My mother was, and she told me that he said if it wouldn't have been for him knowing my mom, he would have shot me right there if I would have answered the door. Only because he knows who my mother and a friend of the family Rocky was, was the reason he didn't come after me anymore. Even though I was wrong for trying to set him on fire for what he thought was just harmless flirting, him saying those inappropriate things to me was harmful to my psyche. I couldn't understand why men thought it was okay for them to talk to me in a disrespectful way. My teenage years were so confusing to me and at this stage, I was still crawling and trying to learn about life, making mistakes and trying to learn from them. I didn't want to make a mistake that would be detrimental to my growth process. However, the road I was headed down my growth didn't look obtainable.

Sj Conerly

Stage Two
The Caterpillar

making mistakes and trying to learn from them. I didn't want to make a mistake that would be detrimental to my growth process. However, the road I was headed down my growth didn't look obtainable.

Sj Conerly

Stage Two
The Caterpillar

Chapter Six
Uncertainty and Unknown

Uncertainty, *the state of being uncertain. Something that I am uncertain of or that causes one to feel uncertain………*

Unknown, *not known or familiar. Undisclosed, untold, dark, hidden, secret……….*

I'm beginning this stage with words that I heard people say about me and how it affected me in different ways I didn't know until I got older. I only picked a couple of words because I could write a whole book about the words that people defined me with and how I began to define myself.

These words became normal for me to hear. I remember the saying sticks and stones may hurt my bones, but words will never hurt me. I wondered who made up that saying because words hurt, as if you got stung by a thousand bees. I didn't fully understand until I got older how some of these words would play a major supporting role in my life. I had already learned to hold things inside and not to show that the hurtful words that people said to me affected me when it did. I'm defining the way these words made me feel.

****

Words of a broken girl grow up with me

Disrespectful, Showing lack of respect or courtesy; impolite………
Scornful, rude, bad-mannered………
   Being disrespectful came along as I became an adolescent. I remember always trying to get family, teachers, police, etc. to listen to what I was trying to say. I was always over-talked. It was as if I was invisible. So, when I started cursing, I got everyone's attention.

Scared of Butterflies

From then on, I would curse when I was being talked over. It then grew into me cursing everybody out. Some adults disrespected me in so many ways, and not just with talking over me. The way adults talked to me, mistreated me and the inconsideration for me as a child was unthinkable. So, the disregard I had for people was a learned behavior but, I liked that I was being heard now. How could I respect authority when I learned from some of them? One of the sayings I would hear, "adults are always right, you are a child so, stay in a child's place, a child doesn't have no wants." I believe those sayings was to excuse their behavior, to make it okay to talk to and hurt children, and make it right on the adults' end, when they would disrespect a child or mentally, physically, verbally or emotionally abuse them. As a child, you couldn't tell an adult they were lying on you because it would be told to you that you were being disrespectful. As I started to grow, I had to unlearn behaviors, as you will read later in this book.

Sj Conerly

Nothing, Not anything or a single thing;
Having no prospect of progress; of no value.........

I felt as if I was the number zero. I couldn't see, I couldn't hear, I was a mute. I felt like someone with no voice that couldn't utter a word. I was conscious of my implied life. I wondered why I couldn't be saved from a lift of pain; there was no hope for me I felt. I was told that I was too far gone and that I didn't want parental guidance. Although, that was far from the truth. I was screaming for an adult in my life to come along and give me guidance and advice that could help me through my difficulties. Someone that would guide me straight when I needed it. There was no one that I could look to for advice or inspiration. Most adults' advice was tearing me down with words, wounding me on the inside. Those wounds never showed up physically, but my behavior and my mental state showed it. I was suffering deeply. Words full of destruction that left wounds on the inside that felt as if they penetrated my veins. No progression,

I guess, was what they thought when it came to me. However, maybe their words were fueled by their past hurts.

Challenging, testing one's abilities; demanding...... Difficult, tough, hard..........

As a young girl, I was called challenging. I would fight about everything. I would challenge your every word. I was trying to demand my respect, even if it was me disrespecting you.

I never started challenging myself unless it was when I was running track and when I thought I wanted to be a hair stylist. Once I discovered my love for writing, I really challenged myself to be something, but even with that it was a struggle. I was depressed and writing at the same time, and it sometimes wasn't easy. Although, I felt the happiest from writing. My big challenge was with me. Me knowing it's okay to become successful, it's okay to be challenging when it was for my good. I had to stop putting challenging together as if it was when I was a young girl getting into lots of trouble. It's okay to be challenging when it's for a greater purpose.

Whore, Prostitute, promiscuous woman, sex worker, call girl……

Prostitute oneself, sell one's body, sell one's self, solicit work in sex industry………

    Whore. I'd been called this word since I was ten years old. I never once sold my body for money. Having people that didn't know me call me this word was mentally damaging to me as a young girl. I wanted to understand at that age why people would assume I was a whore.

    As I got older, I had a cousin say she thought I was a whore. I wondered if someone told that to her daughter, how she would have felt. At that time, I wasn't in a good place mentally; it made me dislike my cousin for years. However, once I started working on my mental state I let that dislike for her go because it was more about me not allowing the effect of hurtful words to continue to affect my mental state. That person wasn't losing sleep over the fact that she felt the need to tell me she thought I was a whore. I put too much energy into how people defined me. As you will read later, I started to change my way of thinking and what I put my energy into.

Fear, an unpleasant emotion caused by the belief that someone or something is dangerous, likely to cause pain, is a threat………

Worry, distress, nervousness, suspicion……….

Fear, crippled me more times than I really wanted to admit it; it had a hold on my life that I wouldn't move. It felt as if my mind was in this conscious coma. Fear almost stopped me from writing this book.

Being so young and knowing that you feared things that didn't have anything to do with scary movies or creepy scrawling things, it was life. And I hadn't started to begin living. When does life start to show its beautiful colors, when does it stop being blue? I would think, when would I learn to be free and not stressed at this age? When would an adult come along and give me some guidance that I needed? When would I stop being the talk of my family in a negative way, when would I grow so I could take care of myself? When, just when? I had lots of questions to ask, but really no one to talk to. I was afraid of being judged more than what I already was. I wanted to stop being afraid that I would be hurt. I wondered what fear looked like. Did it have a certain look or touch? Was it just a figment of my imagination or from the last scary movie I'd seen? I was tired of thinking that someone was out to get me. Life being good to me was something I feared a lot. I know that sounds crazy but when your life is full of abuse and negativity, that's what you are accustomed to. I feared living, I feared normalcy.

Stagnated.........

No growth, no progress, no advancing, or not moving forward.

I was in the same position. Mentally, physically, and spiritually. Not making the changes in life that I needed, to not be hindered. Things were not flowing smoothly; everything felt dull and not full of life. I knew I was just going around in circles with no progress in my life. Just looking at the same things happen with each year.

Words, these negative words were like a beating heart of life destruction. When you hear negative words so much you start to believe them. My dialogue started to become the same as what I had heard for so long. People wanted to keep me in a box of how they perceived and saw me. I believed sometimes people who judged me were looking through a blackened window of a world unknown of endless nothings, not putting a thought into it of why I was the way that I was, and what could have happened in my life, besides me being a fatherless child with a mother that was on drugs. These words grew up with me, fueling me as an adult with a lack of hope and confidence in myself and my life. These words grew roots, rooted words from my childhood, from people that thought they were helping me in their own way. Because of being sexual, verbally, physically and mentally abused, those rooted words hurt me and I hurt people in my life. A life cycle of hurt passing down from one generation to the next, leaving its presence known for years.

The caterpillar stage can be the stage of uncertainty and the unknown. I was at a point in my young life where I lacked confidence and I had low self-esteem; that's the way I saw myself as a teenager. I was always judged in some way or another. Being very young, hearing things from adults that were supposed to be the ones guiding me in the right way was crippling. I was losing the movement of my legs, losing my heart that gave me the energy to fuel the power that came through my legs. Running gave me life when everything around me was dying. Women scorned me because I was a young girl with a body of a woman; back then, I didn't understand why women's perception of me was in a negative way.

Scared of Butterflies

I was called a whore by lots of them, only because my backside was big and not only that, in their minds, I guess, I was having sex with lots of guys, which was not the truth. I was being broken by people that didn't know me, that did know me. So how could I fight against so many people that seemed as if they were born just to destroy me on the inside? My untold truth, I kept with me. I didn't trust people as much anymore and as an adolescent, everything and persons around me, I *wasn't sure if I* could fully trust them with the dark side of my unspoken truth. So, I went deeper inside of me, which wasn't healthy for my mental state of mind.

Chapter Seven
Stop Blaming Myself

Self-blaming, *is a cognitive process in which an individual attributes the occurrence of a stressful event to oneself.........*

🦋 I was very close to one of my little cousins and I always wanted to set a good example for her, and I thought I was. I didn't do things that were crazy around her and I never let her know what I was doing, especially if it was wrong. I was overly protective of her; however, I just wanted the best for my favorite little cousin. If anyone would pick on her they knew once I found out, we were going to fight. Win or lose, I was ready for battle no matter what. It's true that your younger family sometimes looked up to you. I thought I did everything, so she wouldn't be anything like me. I encouraged her, I whipped her little butt when she did wrong, but she wasn't a bad kid, so she very seldom got a whipping from me. She was my little chocolate drop, someone that could never do wrong. But even with me doing everything I did to try and protect her, she followed right behind me and got into a relationship with an older man that wasn't good for her. That hurt me a lot and I blamed myself; that was something I was good at.

Blaming myself for everything that happened in my life, no matter if I had no control of the situation.

Self-blaming for the way other people's lives are or turn out to be is not in your control, unless you have a direct hand in hurting someone. If that is the case, take full responsibility for your actions, even if you don't remember. Don't take away that person's truth, because if what they're saying is true, your memory of what happened will slowly come back to you.

Two people can go through the same door in

life and come out with two different outlooks on the other side of the exit. So, what you may have experienced doesn't mean that person had the exact same experience as you did. Self-blame can be a weapon of mass destruction to your body internally. My emotions and behaviors showed that blaming myself contributed to more self-harm to my already stressful life. I was always ready for war, it seemed like, ready to fight battles that didn't make any since most of the times. Ready to take the anger that was inside on the world. I needed to drill through the innermost core of every part of me to allow myself to be vulnerable, letting down walls so I could allow God to work through me and enter a place within my inner core that I didn't want to go. When would I get to a place in my life that I would be able to not allow things in my life to have some much control over my thoughts. If I wasn't depressed and something happened in my life that didn't go as planned or something happened that I shouldn't have given a second thought, it would send me in a place that was dark, noisy and full of voices talking, repeating the same things over and over. Those voices wouldn't allow me to sleep. I would be locked in the bathroom all night. It was as if I was in a black hole trying to climb out. Sometimes I would make it out but most times I would sink deeper and deeper in that blackened hole full of misery. I wasn't happy. I knew I wanted to be, but I didn't know how to get there. I wished the sun would shine on my life, that I would grow wings and fly.

Chapter Eight
Identity Crisis

Identity-Crisis, *a period of uncertainty and confusion in which a person's sense of identity become insecure, typically do to change in their excepted aims or role in society.*

Most people that know me never knew that I was dealing with things like this. I didn't like when I had the thoughts. Me being told at a very, very young age that I was going to be gay, it really messed with me as a child. I knew I liked boys. Yes, I was a tomboy, but I didn't like girls.

I was only told that because I would be talking to my friend Jenny. She was the only friend I had. No other children would play with me like she did. Labeling, wasn't the way to go about things. Even though I'm not gay, I struggled in that area in life because I heard it so much. When relationships didn't work out, I would say maybe because it's not working out, I'm gay. Or maybe because men keep hurting me, maybe I was gay, or because I would go long periods of time without dating, maybe I'm gay. I know you may think okay, just because someone says that to you, you shouldn't give it a second thought. I was only eight or nine years old. I was a little girl having to deal with my identity because someone wanted to push the way they were on me.

Words can grow up with children so, I believe that you should watch the words that part from your lips because words play a major part in someone's life, no matter if they are good or bad. Words of negativity put me in a shell hiding within myself.

Stage Three
Chrysalis

Chapter Nine
Pupa the Transition

Transition, *the process or a period of changing from one state or condition to another.*

The stage of no growth.

At this stage, a caterpillar is fully grown and would stop eating, but we as a human species continue to grow and learn, but it also depends on the person. Some of us allow life's lessons to stop their growth process I was one of those people. I allowed everything that happened in my life to stagnate my growth, and I wasn't enjoying this journey of life.

No growth = you're stuck treading on water.

I had no motivation for the big dreams that I had inside. I was in a circle living the same life cycle of negative thoughts, no faith in myself or God. I believed the negative things family said about me.

Sj Conerly

When people I didn't know said negative things about me, it didn't affect me in the same way that it did when it was family. My process with trusting family and them loving me and being truly genuine to me, was lacking.

When someone says they love you, you can feel it. Love is an action word and I couldn't differentiate the difference in my growth process to become a butterfly.

As a human species, we're still growing and learning ourselves as we get older, or we can be like the Monarch butterfly that dies after they lay their eggs. Just thinking about that butterfly had me thinking, will I keep allowing myself to slip deeper into depression, or will I continue to allow my soul to die when God wants me to live, but he gives us free will to make choices. Will I make decisions that are best for me, or will I continue to feel sorry for myself, or will I start to make the necessary steps to become a better me.

Bettering myself was something that I always wanted, I was just used to me as I was. I felt trapped in my world that would play out in my head. I felt as if I would never be able to grow to transcend into my authentic self. At this stage, at times I didn't trust myself with myself, or my mental capability to work on myself alone. I had to get professional help through therapy. I was taught to just pray and everything will get better. I know God can help, but when my mind was always all over the place, I couldn't hear God. I didn't want to be judged because I went and talked to a professional, or to be thought as crazy because of it. I continuously put too much thought into what people had to say about me. That was something I knew I had to change if I wanted to be able to grow and the voices to stop playing what people thought of me over and over in my head.

I can remember when I first started to recognize I was depressed was when the father of my children went to jail. I didn't know how to handle that he wouldn't be in my life and on the other hand, I was relieved the years of him cheating and the abuse would be over.

In our almost eight-year relationship, we didn't have healthy arguments without it turning physical or almost turning physical. It got to the point that when we argued, and I thought he was about to hit me, I would hit first sometimes. I was tired of being so aggressive physically because I was so used to him hitting me and abuse alone from men starting with me at a young age. I was tired of the unhealthy relationship with him. Though he started changing and the abuse and cheating stopped, the love I once had for him had already start to change. I would pray to God to take him out of my life, so I guess that was God's way of answering my prayers, when he went to jail. I was sad that he did, but I needed a change. I needed to grow and learn who I was as a woman, mother, sister and friend. Being with him did things to me mentally that I didn't know affected me at the time.

Being so young when I met him was damaging to me growing into a butterfly. My metamorphosis, my life cycle. The relationship wasn't right. It should not have happened, but God allowed things to happen. I had two beautiful children from it and gained beautiful relationships with some of his other children, so I would never say that I regretted being with him. If I was older, that would have been different. So, if the relationship wouldn't have happened I wouldn't have my beautiful daughter and son, or the long friendships with his children and their beautiful children, my grandchildren. I like our family dynamic and even though we are blended we are one family full of love. I went through a lot with him; however, I want to thank him for allowing himself to be vulnerable and allow God to lead his heart and apologize to me. I know personally that apologizing to someone you hurt or didn't know that you hurt, or the relationship wasn't healthy and had an effect on their life or maybe the words you chose to use that broke them, whatever it was that occurred within the relationship, it isn't easy to apologize, especially when it came from the heart. The person that you're apologizing to may not be ready to accept it or may not be in a good place in their life that they're not ready to heal from whatever it is you did to them, or they still think you are the same person you once were. Are maybe they're not reciprocal to your apology because they are not ready to heal from whatever it was that you done to them or what hurt life have given them. So, you can't force people to forgive as long as you forgive for your healing alone.

****

    I had to learn to forgive myself, and that was hard for me. I had to be able to move on because I didn't want to allow those situations to stagnate my progress. Healing takes time and healing of the mind and heart is very important to get to the next level in

Scared of Butterflies

your life. I had to learn that sometimes I had no control over certain things that happened, even when it didn't go the way you planned. For example, you can make a schedule of how you planned to do things in a week. When it doesn't go the way you expected it, know that you tried. Just like asking for forgiveness when it doesn't go the way you excepted it to go. The way you played it over and over in your head how it might go, and it doesn't. Move on, because your subconscious will replay it like your favorite movie, recreating those same thoughts of why it didn't go the way you thought it would. You don't want to allow someone who's not ready to move on or in a state of denial to get you back to negative thoughts, no matter if it only lasts a minute or hour. We are the ones that have control over our time in a day, so don't allow negativity to keep you in a state of no growth. Not growing is like a cancer that can kill every thought of growth; it could be so detrimental to your butterfly affect. Since I was used to the negative thoughts and because negativity was something I always heard from childhood, it was easy to put myself down, and the voices I heard amplified my negative thoughts about me.

Trying to transform into this new being wasn't easy for me. It took a lot of arduous work to get to a healthier mindset. To be honest, I gave up more times than I tried. Giving up was easy because I didn't have to try or put forth any effort for my healing. I didn't have to deal with the tough issues of the hurt in my life, I didn't have to work through the pain I had inside. I needed my past to be resurrected so I could allow God to work on the core of me. Therefore, I could begin the stages of development, so I could have clear and complete thoughts.

Chapter Ten
Life's Cycles

Life Cycle, *the stages a living thing goes through during its life. In some cases, the process is slow, and the changes are gradual. Humans have various steps during their lives.*

A butterfly goes through four stages in its life cycle. I believe people do too. It doesn't take a butterfly long to finish its life cycle; it only takes from a month to a year. As for people, our process takes way longer. We have eighteen years to become what the world says is an adult. Those eighteen years are precious. You're growing and learning yourself and what you want to do with your life. Growing up, your teen years can be trying years; you're developing. In those years, your parents are supposed to nurture you. If you had a plant that you watered every day and gave it lots of light, then it would grow no matter the process. My process of nurturing never happened past eight years old. I wasn't getting the love that I needed, the mother daughter talks I never got, I was never daddy's little girl. Knowing you have a father but didn't know him, hurt deeply. My mother was never supportive and growing up with her was rough. Getting molested and raped at a very young age and hiding it was my stages in life, my process that kept me in a cocoon, my chrysalis, locked in a small, dark, colorless place. I've been hiding my secret for so many years and now that I'm in a place that I want to talk about it, it's scary. Letting people know what really happened to me was something that I wanted to keep hidden, but now that people knew made me uneasy. I can remember a really close family member told a friend of ours I started having sex at ten years old. Because I was so ashamed of what happened to me, I didn't tell her any different. I wondered why my family told our friend that about me, even though she didn't know I got raped. I wondered why someone was worried about who they thought I willingly had sex with at ten years old. I didn't give myself to that young man. I was raped, was what I wanted to say. If it was me, I would have been questioning is he in jail from having sex with her at ten. If my family that was close to me thought I was having sex at ten years old, she was very wrong and maybe had some mental issues herself. I just pretend that it didn't affect me, when I was really screaming on the inside. And at this point, I was tired of all of this old stuff that kept running through my mind. I had the ability to hide things that were hurting me, and I didn't show emotions because I didn't want to deal with the process of healing from those old wounds. I've been depressed for so long, for about a little over twenty years. I made a pretend world and whenever I didn't want to deal with life's process, I would lock myself in the bathroom and it would just be me and my world. This is a poem I

Sj Conerly

wrote called Mirrors, that reflects how I felt:

I'm in a dark place, really dark space
Closed in, hiding from the world
but most of all, me
Scared of the mirrors on the wall,
dreams fall, doors close, as
the storm pushes through the door,
mirrors fall so un-pretty
Loneliness, loveless, heartless
the storm screams
So scared of beautiful
So scared of the true me
That's why I hide from the
mirrors on the wall
because they know just why
I hide from me….

Hiding from the true me was hurting me

internally. I camouflaged by putting on fake smiles and pretending to be happy. I've been depressed over twenty years; pretending was killing me on the inside. I started to gain more and more weight. I knew I needed a change. I couldn't stay like this. If nobody knew, God knew I was putting on. He knew that I had to want to do the work of healing. I knew fear was keeping me from it. Even though I wrote a novel A Tastee Tale, I was depressed the whole time I wrote it. Not wanting to take those steps to becoming a better me was affecting my mental state more and more. The depression was getting harder for me to come out of. I was scared to go outside. The only reason I would go out was if it was for my children to make groceries or it would really have to be important for me to go outside. I was protected in my house; nothing or no one could hurt me. I feared everything that didn't have to do with my pretend world because in it, I was protected. I had the perfect life in my perfect, pretend world. Even though it was false, it was my protection when the real world was ugly to me. When my process was getting hard, when I couldn't come out the depression, my chrysalis was just what I thought I needed at this point in my life, but I wasn't healing. I was that little ten-year-old girl stuck in my past as a woman with no growth, and it was time for me to keep continuing my transition into the woman that I knew I would be and that God created me to be. My colors will show all around me, and I will walk in my purpose.

Scared of Butterflies

Butterfly Affect

Chapter Eleven
The effect affected

Effect, *a change which is a result or consequence of an action or other cause.*

Affect, *influenced or touch by an external factor.*

The effect of abuse and how it affected my relationships in my life varied. I never wanted to hurt people in my life, but it did happen. I didn't know that I hurt certain people in my life. The words of a broken girl grew up with me as I became a woman and I may not have use those same words, but I learned a learned behavior. How could I allow myself to get so deep in depression that I hurt people close to me with words when I got hurt in that way in my life?

On my way home one day, the ride seemed

long as I listened with an open heart and mind at how I hurt someone that I loved dearly. The person that she was telling me about, I didn't know who that person was. I never knew that I hurt her with words. To hear how I, that hurt little girl, grew up into a woman and continued the hurt that was placed inside of me, that made me very uneasy with myself. So uneasy that I had to take in the painful words that she said I told her; some of those same words were told to me. The hurt of that little girl hurt others. I said things that made her feel the same way people made me feel. That talk allowed me to open my eyes more about relationships that were healthy or toxic. The day we talked, neither of us spilled out words that could have caused more hurt.

    I felt that day she got closure. I felt that she really loved me despite that broken person that once hurt her. Later, I found out that she had already forgiven me and had her closure years before that talk. God only knew that I needed her in my life. And

I would soon find out that she needed me too. I was happy that we could continue to be in each other's lives.

The hard part was forgiving myself for that hurt that I caused. The effect of abuse affected my close circle, so I knew that everyone that encountered me in my dark times may have been impacted in some shape or form.

My attitude sometimes was nasty, and I knew that. That was something I wanted to change and that I'd been working on. People that encountered me in my youth and as I started maturing into a woman got different sides of me, which I recently found out by asking some people that knew me in my past and present. At times, I was all over the place. I didn't know which way was up or down, was I coming or going.

Most of my days was fluid with negativity. The effect of abuse hurt so many people around me. Finding out that I hurt people closest to me was a big eye opener for me on relationships and rebuilding them. Rebuilding relationship with my children was something I didn't know that I needed because I didn't think that they were affected by my mental illness, but each one of them were affected in different ways, even if they didn't remember. I wasn't emotionally available for them at times because of the depression and the post dramatic stress order. As I started to go to therapy, I began to become a better mother and friend.

As I was rebuilding relationships there was one relationship that I wanted make things right with for a long time. Our friendship was impaired by others, but because I was so broken and immature I couldn't see the truth behind their negativity because negativity and I were best friends too. I did things to him that a friend shouldn't do. He doesn't believe a friend should hurt a friend and I don't believe it should ever get physical at any point within a friendship so, we both agreed on that. He felt he was being bullied and that is his truth and his truth hurt me because I was the one that hurt him. You should never take away someone's experience with you because everyone that encounters you may experience a different side of you especially when you are a hurt person. Because I really valued him as a person and I love him so much I reached out to him to mend the relationship or at less give him that closure.

After twenty years of being apart, I found out that, that broken girl (me), my effect affected my best friend in a hurtful way. Even though he loved me, he had to let the relationship go back then as teenagers and because I was hurt and not growing, I allowed our relationship to stay non-existent throughout the years. The trust in the relationship had been broken between the both of us and because at that time in my life I was learning how to repair relationships, I didn't know how to go about it because I was unsuccessful with rebuilding relationships. Most

Scared of Butterflies

situations would become so toxic I had to let them go and allow God to work on the issues and move on with my life. However, he was different. I loved him and our friendship even more now. I thank God for the friends that I do have they love me no matter my stubbornness at times; they love me, and I love them.

Throughout my life, I had healthy and unhealthy relationships. They all affected me in some shape or form. One thing I did know, was that I learned from each one of them. I learned I had to let go of the unhealthy relationships and keep the ones that were growing.

My progress with healthy relationships has taught me to appreciate life and the people around me that love me, that will tell me the truth and no matter my flaws, their love for me never changes.

Chapter Twelve
The Great Pretender

Pretend, not really what it is represented as being. To speak and act to make it appear that something is the case when in fact it is not………

Pretender, me. I only depicted what I wanted people to see. I hid my depression for years. Who wants anyone to know that they are depressed? Judgement was what I thought about people not really understanding depression. Nevertheless, I was taking steps to heal, but on the days that I had struggles, I really didn't like to talk about them because I was always misunderstood in some way. I would be told I needed to get over it or stop talking about what I went through, even if it helped someone else to be strong enough to tell what happened to them or get professional help.

That's when the great pretender emerged.

When I wasn't having good days, to keep it in, I had to pretend in front these people because they would think I was handcuffed to my past. I thought about what has the great pretender did for me?

As I was speaking and acting as if I was totally helping my healing, was that getting me any closer to becoming a butterfly? My colors had started to change, and I saw a lot of self-growth, so why pretend for family and friends?

In my chrysalis stage, I learned that I wasn't everyone's cup of tea. I was transforming from immature to maturity. I could admit that I had to grow up in some areas in my adult life. I was somewhat still immature about the way that I handled certain situations with friends and family. I would often blow up and lose any credibility that I was growing, but proving not only to them but to me, myself and I that I was immature when handling some situations. Even though some of them would intentionally provoke me; you will read about triggers and provoking in stage four. I still had to hang myself from a twig leaf like the caterpillar and spin myself into a silky, shiny chrysalis. While I was in my protective covering.

I had to let my old self die and allow a new existence to emerge; therefore, I could continue to go through this ultimate transformation if I wanted to continue to grow while in this stage.

Chapter Thirteen
Struggling

Struggling, striving to achieve or attain something in the face of difficulty or resistance.........

Turning my negative into a positive was something foreign to me. I didn't know where to start; everything was so confusing. I was trying to do something that I'd never really put too much effort into. With the words turning a negative into a positive keep playing through my mind, the more I wanted to change and my thoughts about the words, the more I felt I would never achieve that goal of positivity. I needed to change that around.

I remember a conversation I had with a friend of the family, thinking I would get some encouragement. I was deep in my emotions and I let my mouth say what my heart was feeling and that was a new feeling for me. I allowed myself to be defenseless. I touch on my life and what happened to me my mom, my dad, the molestation and rape.

 As the conversation progressed, I was told that I was having a pity party, amongst other things that were said to me, not one encouraging word. I was told one thing that I probably needed to hear at that time. That she knew people that grew up like I did and went through things that I did, and they still made something out of their lives. So, what was it that they did that I didn't? Even though I knew the person I was talking to wasn't telling me that for me to feel better about myself, I knew it wasn't coming from a good place, it was to make me feel even worse, but God knew what I needed to hear at that time. So, those words that were told to me, I had to make them work for me in a positive way.

 Turning a negative into a positive was like doing a very difficult equation for me, and I never was really good at math. It wasn't as simple as one plus one equals two. With math, it's something that you must work hard at to learn. Turning this negative into a positive for me was as if I was going to school to become a mathematician. I needed to work on the small equations first, even though those smaller equations were more difficult than calculus. Building closer relationships with my children and going through that I needed to be present mentally for them, my friends and immediate family; other family members will have to come at a later time in my life. At this moment, it was about me.

Because I wanted to come out this chrysalis with new colors and a different way of hearing and seeing things. Healing from some relationships was letting some go too.

Chapter Fourteen
Growing Mentally and Letting Go

The Red- Spotted Purple butterflies like to sit on rotting fruit. In my life, I held on to things that were old that needed to be disposed of. Holding on to those old things wasn't good for me; it rooted everything around me with negativity. Even when I tried changing my negative state of mind, but I wasn't really putting a lot of effort into my progress. I wasn't going to the therapy that I needed, I wasn't praying either. Therefore, my mindset was the same and negativity was attracted to me, even if it wasn't coming from me. It took me many years to really get to a healthy state of mind because I was holding on to the rotting fruit and I had to continue to give into the process of growth fully.

Chapter fifteen
Levels

Levels, *a horizontal plane or line with respect to the distance above or below a given point.*

I always wanted to get to that next level in life. My mental state and fear encumbered me in my career. It was as if I was standing at the edge of a cliff and to get to the that next level, all I had to do was jump, but fear was always standing behind me pulling me more than two steps back. Being at that stage where I knew my chrysalis wasn't where I needed to be. I needed to be in the real world full of words, art, music and everything that kept me inspired. And that was amongst people, places and things, not in a world in my head that kept me from growing.

Scared of Butterflies

For so many years, that world kept me from really seeing the blessings of God. With all the horrible things that I went through, I felt at one point I needed to live in my head, but I knew it was unhealthy and I wanted to be mentally healthy.

Brokenness, hurt, fear and what people had to say or thought of me, I wear it like armor. My voice spoke of it, my body language showed it, my heart embraced it. Negativity followed me like a thief in the night. It was leashed on to every fiber of my body. My blood boiled from it, my soul cried because of it, but I didn't need it. I was trapped like an animal in the zoo that needed to be released into the wild. I wasn't able to achieve the things I wanted to do in life when I kept the same thought process of what happened to me and because of that, it kept me bound. I needed to forgive the men who raped me, broke my heart, physically, mentally and emotionally abused me, but to do that I had to forgive the man that first hurt me, and that was my father. I had to forgive him for abandoning me, for acting as if I didn't exist, for him not showing me how a man should treat a woman, for him not being there to dry my tears when I just wanted him. For just never having a chance to be daddy's little girl. I had to forgive my mother for not being there to nurture me, for her allowing whatever happened to her in life to affect how I was treated and our relationship. I had to forgive myself for the self-harm I'd done to myself, for allowing myself to go so many years without getting help. I had to forgive me for not being emotionally available to my older children, for hurting them, for hurting people that were close to me. Forgiveness was the key to my freedom; it was my pathway to living life.

In addition, being homeless with my children taught me that life isn't going to go the way you think, and not to worry about things that you have no control over. That was one of my biggest problems; worrying about everything. One thing I do believe

Scared of Butterflies

because of this homeless season in my life, I started to grow more than I could see myself doing. I felt different, but I didn't know it was growth at the time because I was dealing with life. I had to continue to get rid of the rotted things in my life, so I could continue the growth process. I learned you will worry somethings but pray about it all. With this passage from the Bible laid on my heart, I was able to get through things I had no control over. And I had to forgive myself for not providing what my children needed at that time. Forgiving myself and letting go of the things I couldn't control brought me a lot of peace in my life. I never wanted the peace that was in my heart and mind to ever be disturbed again. Praying a lot helped me in my life.

Philippians 4:6-7
Do not be anxious about anything, but in everything, by prayer and petition, with thanksgiving, present your requests to God. And the peace of God,

Sj Conerly

which transcends all understanding, will guard your hearts and your minds in Christ Jesus.

Scared of Butterflies

Stage Four
Butterfly

Chapter Sixteen
Outcome

Outcome, *the way things turn out; consequence*

The butterfly develops through a process called metamorphosis, which means transformation or change in shape. I defiantly had transformed into an angry person because my life was reshaped by those unfortunate events that happened in it. Becoming a butterfly was scary for me. I thought of everything that could go wrong or right. I feared the things that could go right the most. I was used to the things going wrong and hurtful things.

I was scared of succeeding.

Afraid of God's promise.

Afraid of becoming that greater being.

To become a better being I had to become one with my mind, body and spirit. In addition, by me changing the trivial things in my life, by doing that, I was changing the total outcome of my life. Although I had gotten my wings, sometimes I was afraid to fly. I still had some old demons I had yet to deal with. It was a time in my life I didn't want my mother to be my mother and my father to be my father. What if I wasn't born to my parents? I wouldn't be me, I wouldn't be the writer that I am today. You wouldn't be reading this book. I wouldn't exist. I believe if God wanted that, I wouldn't have been born. I was wishing my total existence away. I had really started loving myself no matter who my parents were or what my background was.

My butterfly affect changed the outcome in my life. I was born to a mother that turned to drugs to numb whatever hurt she experienced. My father was a pastor who had many children and was abandon by his mother and he was abandon me. I'm sure my parents' metamorphoses changed their lives. I knew they didn't have a really good childhood;

therefore, I was hurt by it. However, their journey to become butterflies wasn't smooth; they had to grow just like I did. We all have a story, some good, some bad. Just know whatever decision we make can change the overall outcome in our life, good or bad.

Even though my outcome in life started out hard, me wishing I had a new life wasn't helping my issues. They were still there no matter how hard I had wished. However, once I got the tools that I needed to navigate through my challenges and stop wishing that who God intended for my parents to be wasn't, I was able to deal with the important things in life. Really allowing God to come in and lead me in the way that he wanted me to go, my outcome started to change in a positive direction.

.

Chapter Seventeen
Labels and Lessons

Labels, *a small piece of paper, fabric, plastic, or similar material attached to an object and giving information about it.........*
Lesson, *an amount of teaching given at one time; a period of learning or teaching.........*
Keep your labels.........

Labels and lesson in this life can sometimes be taken the wrong way. I was labeled more often than I wanted to be in my life. Lessons in life can teach you something, crossing paths with the many different people that I have in my short thirty-eight years on this earth.

Once, I was told that I thought God saved you from that, and that was me defending myself, but because some people were used to me handling situations in the wrong way. Even if I handled it as calm as I could, they would still see it the way they wanted to. I was looked at in the worst way possible when it came to judgement and putting labels on me. So, I wanted my spicy side to disappear and never to return to try and please others, when that's a part of who I am. I can remember having no voice, people always jumping to conclusions before listening to what I had to say. I knew I had to change things about me. Everyone knows when they need personal growth. Some don't like to admit when they need to change, some people do, and some people will never change; they will be stuck in the same cycle of no growth, immaturity and negativity. Their thought process will stay the same, how they think about you and themselves. I just had to choose to regain my life and not worry about what people thought of me and all the labels that were assigned to me by others. I had to learn to unassign there labels by having better thoughts about myself and regaining my self-esteem, starting within first so that I could become colorful like a butterfly.

I've learned that you must take the good with the bad because you will always have people that label you and judge you. No matter if you're doing good or bad, people are going to be people. Love them with the love of God and move on. You can't allow your mind to dwell on the negative things. If, you do, it would overtake so much of your time in a day, and you have control of your time. Surround yourself with like-minded people and you will see yourself grow, if you allow it.

Sj Conerly

Chapter Eighteen
Seeing new Colors

Colors, *the property possessed by an object of producing different sensations on the eye as a result of the way the object reflects or emits light………*

Being a butterfly can be beautiful, to spread your wings and soar into the sky. Being able to see the things they see, to fly as high as I possibly could was what I was aiming for. Butterflies are beautiful, their color patterns are unique. It isn't as if you've never seen these colors before, but you must admit when you see a butterfly, it seems like it was your first time, as if it is a foreign species. You want to remember those colors, hang on to those colors as long as you possibly can because of their beauty. I would close my eyes and think of the most beautiful butterfly I'd ever seen. I could feel those colors running

Scared of Butterflies

through my mind through my veins. Butterflies learned to fly fast. As soon as the blood started pumping through their veins; their wings started to flap and flap, than they flew. That easy, I thought. It looks as if they've been waiting for this moment since they were an egg. But this is the stage some people get stuck at. The stage I had been stuck at for many years. I allowed my life's struggles to keep me from flying. I wanted those beautiful colors always, I wanted to move past the hurtful things in my life, but life's events kept coming to drag my past into my present. It seemed when it was my turn to learn to fly, I let my situation, my trials and tribulations stop me from progressing, but not anymore. I was growing, and I liked the feeling of change. I felt that I was becoming my authentic self.

Chapter Nineteen
My Learning Period

Learning, *any relatively permanent change in behavior that occurs as a direct result of experience………*

As my wings began to grow more stronger, I had to stop allowing people to define who I was in my present and started creating my own definition of who I am and who I want to be and the person I was becoming. If I would continue to allow people to keep me in my past of how I used to be, I will never continue to grow. On this journey of transforming into a butterfly, I learned that some people you may have hurt, they were maybe still stuck in the place where you once hurt them. People will love the good qualities in you, but if one time you do something that doesn't fit their picture or whatever their lifestyle is, you were sentenced to a life time of judgement and labeling. Once I accepted myself for who I was with all my imperfections, I was able to grow and love myself more. So, when you are able to love someone with all their flaws, it shows the truth in the action word love. I believe that the most powerful thing you can do is accept a person for who they are. We as a human species are not perfect. We do make mistakes but learning from our mistakes shows our maturity and growth. You are never too old to learn and grow your wings. I was an open vessel that was ready to receive and not block everyone out. I wanted not to feel that everyone was out to get me and always feeling that I was broken and alone. And when that feeling, and thoughts left my body, I felt as if I could fly. As if I was literally a butterfly.

    The learning period never ends. Listening to a lot of uplifting music, speeches and sermons and being around like-minded people helps. One sermon in particular was by Sarah Jakes Roberts. People still talk about me, trying to keep me chained to my past.

Sj Conerly

When I heard her say these words, "God, I just want to bow out gracefully," I thought about when people talked about me to try to break me with words, with what their definition was of me, or trying to keep me restrained to my past.

    I'm learning, I'm learning, I'm learning God to blow out gracefully.

Chapter Twenty
Levels of balance

Balance, in my life was something that I needed but, I didn't know what I needed to get balanced. When my mind was all over the place, I couldn't think straight enough to know what to do to balance my life. I was dealing with my own demons, if that's what you want to call it. When balancing my life, it was as if I was walking on a tight rope, but to get to the other side I had to learn what it was that I needed and didn't need in my life now. One thing I did know was that I wanted to have a clear mind and heart. I thought, how could I allow myself to let this no progressing go on for so long? I was listening to what people had to say and what I should do and what they thought was best for me still, but I was in a deep depression at that time. I was struggling with letting go of what I was used to. Now God did send a person back in my life that was a great friend and that inspired me to do wonderful things in life and encouraged me in my dark times. Even though that person is younger than I am, I've learned when God does place a person in your life for a short period of time or for a lifetime, that it'd be all for a life lesson.

    Everyone's balance may not be the same. The way you balance your life can have various levels to it. My balance levels were being consistent with my mental health, physical health, my relationships with my immediate family and my close friends. I started by getting the mental help that I needed to be able to get my relationships at a better and healthier place than they were. I had to learn to prioritize my life. I set what I needed to do daily so I won't get overwhelmed and over think things. I had to stop making other people problems mine. I had to stop thinking I can help people grow when

Scared of Butterflies

that weren't ready for their own healing and growth. I continue the work that I needed so my balance in my life could stay leveled.

Chapter Twenty-One
Trigger a Butterfly

Growing, you will always have someone that wants to prove that you haven't grown from the old you.

Let's say you have someone in your life that tries to provoke you to behave in a way that you don't like about yourself and that you've been working on. Learning what or who triggers you is one of the first steps to changing your behavior because you are the only one that has control over you.

Using myself for an example, I can't talk or be in the presence of someone that provokes me to anger quick. I'm still learning to control my defective behavior. I need to ameliorate my behavior for me not to prove to anyone that I haven't grown. Getting your wings is for you. No matter how old you are, you are never too old to learn.

Remember there are people out there that know you and the way you react to certain situations, and they will try their hardest to get you out of your character, that they think you still are, just to prove an unnecessary point. That you are the same person you once were. Don't be in the company of people that deliberately provoke you. You have to learn to let those type of people go no matter if they're friends or family. Move on and love them from a distance.

As for as strangers go, they will test the waters just to get you to behave in the way that they want you to. However, you are the only one that has control over you.

Chapter Twenty-Two
Chase life Chances

Chances, *do something despite its being dangerous or of uncertain outcome*.........

Life can be funny when it comes to chances. I never thought that I would see a different life from the one I had. One day something came knocking at my door, and that something was chance. Chance ran me down as if I had stolen something that wasn't mine. What will I do with is what counts the most. Will I continue to allow what I see in front of me to control my path or will I take this God-given opportunity to become a beautiful species? Imagining my life would be something other than what it was, was unimaginable to me at one time, because what I knew wasn't beautiful. I had to start putting beautiful

Scared of Butterflies

thoughts and colors out into the universe because God draped this imperfect world with them, and that God loved me because of them and being able to grow, learn and appreciate yourself with your flaws because we all have them. However, I had to be a willing participant and grab hold to what I felt was my second chance at life. Although, I felt at times in my life I was torn from the inside out when healing from my past. The rain would stop for seasons in my life, but when God sent chance, so I could view things in my life differently other than what I was familiar with, it opened my eyes and mind to colors I hadn't seen before. The way I thought about things started to change. I know I had the same set of eyes, but a different look. It was as if I was looking through a different set of eyes. I still had some struggles in my personal life, but the colors I was seeing weren't the same. I started to see this different species. Bright colors were all around me no matter what I was going through. I started to speak more positive, think positive. I spoke life and not death over my life, my children's lives and my career.

My affect wasn't easy; it was a hard process and still is. I'm still learning to fly. Sometimes I fall but I've learned not to stay there. I've learned that I'm not that young, disrespectful girl that I used to be, that everyone thought was going to be nothing. I'm still growing and learning to go through my butterfly affects but more in a positive way.

I was finally seeing what God had for me. I was believing in me becoming this beautiful species that God had created that I could compare my life to. Make sure that you keep chasing chance because you never know when it will come knocking again.

Chance came knocking at my door and brought along with-it life's beauty and a beautiful creature that God created, a butterfly, and all it's beautiful colors so I can no longer be scared of butterflies.

Things I stand by to become a butterfly

- *Put God first*
- *You will have worries, but pray about them all*
- *Love yourself*
- *Believe in who you are*
- *It's okay to make mistakes. Learn from them*
- *Stay consistent and disciplined*
- *Don't worry about how people define you*
- *Take time out for yourself doing things without your husband, wife or your children is good for your mental health. You can lose yourself basing your life totally for other people*

Acknowledgements

I want to give thanks to all the people that were with me from the beginning. To my children this is for you guys. I love you all. Remember you want to leave your footprints in this world and there is nothing that you can't do because God live in you.

Last, but never least, and the one I give all the praise to God. Thanks for giving me the courage to do this and be free to write in the land of words. For all my trials and tribulations, for all my life's lesson I've learned a lot from them. I thank you, because of them, I'm a stronger and more confident woman.

I want to thank all the readers for supporting me. Remember never give up on you the universe is waiting.

Scared of Butterflies

www.ingramcontent.com/pod-product-compliance
Lightning Source LLC
Chambersburg PA
CBHW020916090426
42736CB00008B/666